WORK AN OCCUPATIONAL ABC

FOR KIERSTEN

Groundwood Books / House of Anansi Press
110 Spadina Avenue, Suite 801, Toronto, Ontario M5V 2K4
or c/o Publishers Group West
1700 Fourth Street, Berkeley, CA 94710

We acknowledge for their financial support of our publishing program the Canada
Council for the Arts, the Government of Canada through the Canada Book Fund (CBF)
and the Ontario Arts Council.

 Canada Council   Conseil des Arts
for the Arts   du Canada

 ONTARIO ARTS COUNCIL
CONSEIL DES ARTS DE L'ONTARIO
an Ontario government agency
un organisme du gouvernement de l'Ontario

Library and Archives Canada Cataloguing in Publication
Hatanaka, Kellen, author
Work : an occupational ABC / Kellen Hatanaka.
Issued in print and electronic formats.
ISBN 978-1-55498-409-1 (bound).—ISBN 978-1-55498-410-7 (pdf)
1. English language—Alphabet—Juvenile literature.
2. Occupations—Juvenile literature. 3. Alphabet books.
I. Title.
PE1155.H38 2014   j421'.1   C2014-900895-3
C2014-900896-1

The illustrations were created digitally, using hand-drawn patterns and textures.
Design by Kellen Hatanaka
Printed and bound in Malaysia

 FSC
www.fsc.org
MIX
Paper from
responsible sources
FSC® C012700

AN OCCUPATIONAL ABC
WORK

KELLEN HATANAKA

GROUNDWOOD BOOKS   HOUSE OF ANANSI PRESS   TORONTO   BERKELEY

AVIATOR

BUTCHER

CYCLIST

DETECTIVE

EXPLORER

FOREST RANGER

GROCER

HORTICULTURALIST

ICE CREAM VENDOR

JOCKEY

K-9 OFFICER

LUMBERJACK

MOUNTAINEER

NAVAL ARCHITECT

OCEANOGRAPHER

POSTAL WORKER

QUARTERBACK

RINGMASTER

SKATEBOARDER

TAILOR

UMPIRE

VIBRAPHONIST

WEDDING SINGER

XENOLOGIST

YOGI

ZOOKEEPER

WANT ADS

AVIATOR
Want a career that will really let you soar? Aviation may be the job for you!

BUTCHER
Do you have a passion for quality meats? Here's a career that's a cut above the rest!

CYCLIST
Get into high gear and pursue a career in professional cycling.

DETECTIVE
Are you a problem solver with a keen eye? Success as a detective is all in the details.

EXPLORER
Do you enjoy investigating the unknown? Discover an exciting career as an explorer!

FOREST RANGER
If you're a nature lover, this job is a walk in the park.

GROCER
If you want a career that's always fresh, the grocery business is for you!

HORTICULTURALIST
You'll never stop growing with a career in horticulture.

ICE CREAM VENDOR
This is a cool job with sweet benefits.

JOCKEY
Being a jockey is a great job for thrill-seeking animal lovers. Saddle up for a career in the fast lane!

K-9 OFFICER
As a K-9 officer, you'll be able to fight crime with your best friend.

LUMBERJACK
Lumberjacks climb, saw and chop down trees. With this active, outdoorsy career, you'll never be a bump on a log!

MOUNTAINEER
Mountaineering is a perfect job for active adventurers who want to take their career to new heights.

NAVAL ARCHITECT
Why not set sail on an exciting career in naval architecture?

WANT ADS

OCEANOGRAPHER
As an oceanographer, you'll have a career you can really dive into!

POSTAL WORKER
Postal workers have the kind of job that always delivers!

QUARTERBACK
If you love sports, this is a tough job to pass up.

RINGMASTER
From organizing clowns to announcing acrobats, this job is a real balancing act.

SKATEBOARDER
Skateboarding is a great job for those who are creative and athletic. Between landing tricks and skating new spots, you'll enjoy the daily grind.

TAILOR
If you like to design, make and alter clothes, then a career as a tailor is well suited to you.

UMPIRE
If you're the type of person who likes to have the final say, being an umpire might fit like a glove.

VIBRAPHONIST
For a career that promises good vibes, consider taking up the vibraphone.

WEDDING SINGER
If you love to sing and entertain, then say "I do" to a career as a wedding singer.

XENOLOGIST
This is a job that's really out of this world.

YOGI
This is a great career for anyone looking for a job with flexibility.

ZOOKEEPER
Zookeeping might be the only job that encourages monkey business.